W9-ARJ-734

The Cheyenne

by Petra Press

Content Adviser: Dr. Bruce Bernstein, Assistant Director for Cultural
Resources, National Museum of the American Indian, Smithsonian Institution

Social Science Adviser: Professor Sherry L. Field,
Department of Curriculum and Instruction, College of Education,
The University of Texas at Austin

Reading Adviser: Dr. Linda D. Labbo,
Department of Reading Education, College of Education,
The University of Georgia

COMPASS POINT BOOKS

Minneapolis, Minnesota

FIRST REPORTS

Compass Point Books
3722 West 50th Street, #115
Minneapolis, MN 55410

Visit Compass Point Books on the Internet at *www.compasspointbooks.com* or e-mail your request
to *custserv@compasspointbooks.com*

Cover: A Cheyenne war bonnet worn by late 19th century Chief Wooden Leg

Photographs ©: Courtesy, Colorado Historical Society, #CHS-X20022, cover; Kit Breen, 4;
Richard Hamilton Smith, 7; Smithsonian American Art Museum, Washington, D.C./Art Resource,
N.Y., 8–9, 10, 23; N. Carter/North Wind Picture Archives, 11; Oregon Trail Museum Association,
13, 24; North Wind Picture Archives, 14–15, 30–31; Bettmann/Corbis, 16; Unicorn Stock
Photos/Mark & Sue Werner, 17; Jan Lucie, 19, 43; Library of Congress, 20; Hulton Getty/Archive
Photos, 22, 25; The Denver Public Library, Western History Collection, 26–27, 28–29, 32; Brian
Vikander/Corbis, 34; Kansas State Historical Society, 35; Corbis, 36–37, 41; Courtesy Museum of
New Mexico, #67683, 38–39; Tom Bean/Corbis, 40; AFP/Corbis, 42.

Editors: E. Russell Primm, Emily J. Dolbear, and Alice K. Flanagan
Photo Researchers: Svetlana Zhurkina and Jo Miller
Photo Selector: Catherine Neitge
Designer: Bradfordesign, Inc.
Cartographer: XNR Productions, Inc.

Library of Congress Cataloging-in-Publication Data
Press, Petra.
The Cheyenne / by Petra Press.
p. cm. — (First reports)
Includes bibliographical references and index.
ISBN 0-7565-0186-5
1. Cheyenne Indians—Juvenile literature. [1. Cheyenne Indians. 2. Indians of North America—
Great Plains.] I. Title. II. Series.
E99.C53 P73 2002
978.004'973—dc21   20010044124

Table of Contents

▲ Steven Little Bird, a member of the Cheyenne and Arapaho tribes, performs a dance.

The People

Most Cheyenne (pronounced shy-AN) live in southern Montana and Oklahoma. There are two branches of Cheyenne Indians—the Northern Cheyenne and the Southern Cheyenne.

The Northern Cheyenne live on the Northern Cheyenne **Reservation** in Lame Deer, Montana. The Southern Cheyenne share land with the Arapaho tribe in Oklahoma.

Long ago, the Cheyenne lived in central Minnesota. They shared land with other Native American tribes. Everyone hunted animals and gathered wild plants.

In the late 1600s, the Cheyenne packed up and moved west. Enemy tribes may have driven them away.

The name "Cheyenne" comes from *Shayiyena*. This Sioux word means "people of the strange

Map labels:

CANADA

Alberta · Saskatchewan · Manitoba · Lake of the Woods · Ont.

Missouri

Montana

Northern Cheyenne Ind. Res.

North Dakota

Minnesota

L. Superior

Mich.

Battle of the Little Bighorn, 1876

South Dakota

Wisconsin

Idaho

Wyoming

Mississippi

Iowa

Illinois

Great Salt Lake

Nebraska

Missouri

UNITED STATES

Utah

Colorado

Colorado

Kansas

Missouri

Sand Creek, 1864

Arizona

New Mexico

Cheyenne and Arapaho Tribes of Oklahoma (headquarters in Concho, Okla.)

Oklahoma

Arkansas

N
W   E
S

Texas

Rio Grande

| 0 | 100 | 200 miles |
| 0 | 100 | 200 kilometers |

Cheyenne lands at time of European contact

Present-day Cheyenne reservation

Battle/attack site

▲ Past and present Cheyenne lands

speech." The Cheyenne call themselves *Tsistsistas*, or "the People."

Life in Minnesota

In 1680, the Cheyenne lived along the Mississippi River in Minnesota. Their houses were earth lodges. They were wood, covered with bark and earth.

Small family groups of Cheyenne farmed and hunted. They grew corn, squash, and beans. They gathered berries, nuts, and potatoes.

▲ *The Cheyenne lived in the forests along the Mississippi River in Minnesota.*

In summer, the Cheyenne collected wild rice. This grain grew along nearby lakes and streams. Women dried the rice over a low fire. Then they stored it to eat during winter.

The men hunted deer, foxes, and squirrels. They also caught fish and turtles from rivers and lakes.

◀ *Minnesota Indians gathered wild rice and hunted.*

The Cheyenne had a good life in Minnesota. But in the early 1700s, they left. The Sioux and Ojibwa, who were also known as the Chippewa, may have forced the Cheyenne out. They followed the Minnesota River to what is now North Dakota and South Dakota. There they built new villages.

On the Great Plains

▲ *The Cheyenne lived in the Missouri River valley, shown here in a painting by George Catlin.*

At first, the Cheyenne built their villages in the Missouri River valley. The weather was good, and food was plentiful on the **Great Plains**.

The men hunted buffalo, bear, elk, deer, antelope, raccoon, and geese. They fished for sturgeon and pike in the rivers. Women grew corn, beans, squash, and tobacco.

The Cheyenne lived in earth lodges, as they had in Minnesota. Sometimes fifteen to thirty related people lived in one lodge.

▲ *The Cheyenne River, which is named after the tribe, goes around the Black Hills in South Dakota.*

During the 1730s, Cheyenne life changed. Europeans had come to the Dakotas to trade and sometimes to live. The Cheyenne traded furs and animal hides for blankets, metal tools, cooking pots, and horses. Soon they also traded for guns.

Horses and guns made life easier for Native Americans. A hunter could travel farther on a horse than he could on foot. He could kill animals more quickly and return home sooner. But horses and guns also made life more dangerous.

Slowly, tribes began to fight over hunting grounds. They also fought over access to trade goods such as guns. In time, the fights turned into wars.

Hunting the Buffalo

By the late 1700s, the Cheyenne stopped farming. Buffalo meat became their main food. They hunted the buffalo on horseback.

▲ *Native Americans hunted buffalo on horseback, as shown in this painting by William Henry Jackson.*

Following the buffalo from place to place made permanent village life difficult. So the Cheyenne left their earth lodges and began living in skin tents called tepees. Tepees were light and easy to move.

The Cheyenne used every part of the buffalo. Women soaked and scraped the skins. Then they dried them in the sun. They used the hides for clothing and tepees.

From the bones of the buffalo, the women carved needles, toys, and tools. From the horns, they made spoons and cups.

▲ *A Native American woman prepares a buffalo hide to make a robe.*

The women braided buffalo hair into ropes. They made soap from the fat. They used the stomach to carry food and water. They dried buffalo droppings to burn for their fires.

The buffalo was very important to the Cheyenne. They treated this animal with great respect. Many of their **ceremonies** honored the spirit of the buffalo. The Cheyenne today continue to honor the buffalo.

◀ *Like many tribes, the Cheyenne honored the spirit of the buffalo.*

▲ *The Cheyenne depended on the buffalo for food and many other things.*

Cheyenne Ceremonies

Today, many Cheyenne people continue to practice their religion. From earliest times, the Cheyenne believed in a Great Spirit named *Maiyun*. Their most important ceremonies honor the Great Spirit.

A long time ago, Maiyun gave the Cheyenne four sacred arrows. They were called the *Mahuts*. Two arrows were for hunting, and two arrows were for war. The Great Spirit gave the people these arrows to guide and protect them.

The Cheyenne kept these sacred arrows in a skin bag called a **medicine bundle**. Every year, the Cheyenne gathered to honor the arrows. They also honored what the arrows stood for.

Even today, the Cheyenne take part in this ceremony to honor the four sacred arrows. They choose a respected member of the tribe to be Keeper of the Sacred Arrows.

▲ *A Cheyenne in Montana performs a traditional dance.*

▲ *A special Sun Dance lodge, as shown in this 1910 picture by photographer Edward S. Curtis*

Another important ceremony is the New Life Lodge, or Sun Dance. Every summer, people celebrate the Sun Dance. Today, as in the past, they build a special lodge with a sacred pole in the center. For a week, they **fast**, pray, and dance around the pole.

A Sun Dance is a time to see family and friends. It is also a time for games and feasts.

In the past, people believed the Sun Dance would bring success in war and hunting. They also thought it would protect the people from sickness and enemies. Today, the Cheyenne pray for health and well-being during the Sun Dance.

In the past, the Sun Dance showed that people were brave enough to become **warriors**. They fasted for several days. Then they danced many hours in the hot sun and prayed to the Great Spirit.

Today, people in the Sun Dance pray and fast. They suffer so that their prayers will be answered. They pray to be able to live good lives as the Cheyenne before them did.

Broken Promises

▲ *This drawing from the 1830s shows a Mandan chief, left, and a Cheyenne chief fighting.*

In the early 1800s, the Cheyenne left the Missouri River valley. They were looking for better hunting grounds.

They traveled through what is today Montana, Wyoming, and Colorado. Along the way, they made friends with the Sioux and Arapaho. They made enemies of the Kiowa and Comanche.

About 1832, the Cheyenne split into two groups. One group stayed along the Platte River in what is now Nebraska. They are called the Northern Cheyenne.

The other group traveled farther south to the Arkansas River in what is today Colorado and Kansas. They are called the Southern Cheyenne.

Before long, white settlers came to the new Cheyenne land, too. Soon Native Americans and settlers were fighting over the land.

In 1851, at Fort Laramie in Wyoming, the Northern Cheyenne and other Plains Indians signed a **treaty** with the U.S. government. The Indians agreed to stop fighting and give up some land.

◄ Cheyenne chief Wolf on the Hill, as painted by George Catlin in 1832

▲ *Travelers on the Oregon Trail, as shown in this painting by William Henry Jackson*

The Indians also promised not to harm Oregon Trail settlers. In return, the government agreed to protect Indian lands from more white settlements.

However, in 1858, gold was discovered in what is today Colorado. Within months, thousands of miners and settlers came. The U.S. government broke its promise and helped take Indian lands.

Three years later, the Cheyenne signed another treaty giving up even more land. This treaty did not keep settlers out of Indian territory, however. More settlers came.

When the Cheyenne fought back, U.S. troops were sent. Sometimes, the soldiers attacked peaceful Indian villages.

▲ *Gold miners in Telluride, Colorado, in the late 1800s*

The Sand Creek Massacre

In 1864, some Cheyenne were camped near Sand Creek in Colorado. The leader, Chief Black Kettle,

U.S. troops killed more than 300 Cheyenne during the Sand Creek Massacre.

wanted peace. A U.S. Army colonel named John Chivington did not care. He wanted them out of the way.

On November 29, 1864, Chivington's soldiers rode into the village. They killed more than 300 Cheyenne.

Most were women and children. The killings became known as the Sand Creek **Massacre**.

Chief Black Kettle escaped during the fighting. Black Kettle tried to keep his younger warriors from fighting. Some joined other tribes, however. He was later killed in a U.S. attack in Oklahoma.

For two years, the Cheyenne, Arapaho, Sioux, Comanche, and Kiowa led **raids** against white settlers in Colorado and Kansas. They wanted to protect their rights, lands, and families.

But the U.S. government had more troops and better weapons. The southern tribes had to give up.

▲ *Chief Black Kettle was killed during an attack on his camp on the Washita River.*

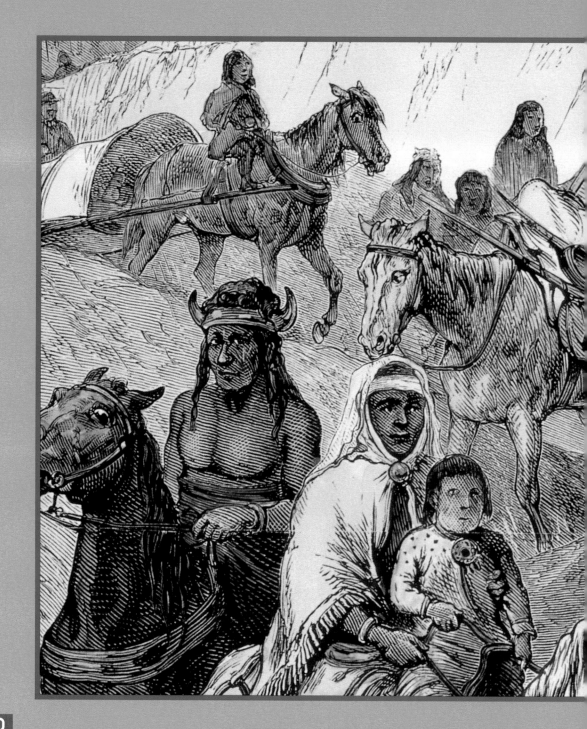

In 1867, the Southern Cheyenne signed the Treaty of Medicine Lodge Creek in Kansas. A year later, they signed a second Fort Laramie Treaty in Wyoming.

The Southern Cheyenne gave up all their land. They were forced to move to Oklahoma. They had to share land with the Arapaho.

In return, the U.S. government promised to give the Southern Cheyenne $500,000. It also promised to provide their people food and clothes for the next twenty-five years.

◄ *The Cheyenne had to move to a reservation in Oklahoma and share land with the Arapaho.*

▲ *Roman Nose, a Cheyenne warrior, led an attack against U.S. troops in 1868.*

The Battle of the Little Bighorn

On the Great Plains, the Northern Cheyenne kept fighting. They joined the Sioux to fight for their homeland. For many years, they battled to keep U.S. troops and settlers away.

Then in 1874, gold was discovered in the Black Hills of South Dakota. It brought more miners and settlers into the area. Angry Cheyenne attacked them, but U.S. troops protected the miners and settlers.

In late June 1876, Sioux and Cheyenne families were camped near the Little Bighorn River in Montana. U.S. general George Armstrong Custer planned to destroy them.

On June 25, 1876, Custer and his soldiers fought the Indians in the Battle of the Little Bighorn. The Native Americans killed Custer and his 225 men. Their great victory did not last long, however. Thousands of new troops were sent.

▲ *Cheyenne and Sioux warriors celebrate their victory during a reenactment of the Battle of the Little Bighorn.*

In 1877, the Northern Cheyenne gave up at Fort Robinson, Nebraska. Later, they were sent to the Cheyenne-Arapaho reservation in Oklahoma.

Reservation Life

The Cheyenne found reservation life very hard. They missed life on the rolling grasslands of Wyoming and Montana. The U.S. government didn't always send the food they had promised. Diseases such as malaria killed many families.

Unable to suffer further injustices, a chief named Dull Knife escaped from the reservation in September 1877. About 300 other Cheyenne joined him.

▲ *Captured members of Dull Knife's band in Dodge City, Kansas, in 1878*

More than 10,000 U.S. troops chased them across the country. They caught them six weeks later. In 1881, after many talks with the U.S. government, the Northern Cheyenne got their own reservation in Montana.

In the early 1900s, the U.S. government wanted Cheyenne land again. A law was passed to help outsiders buy Cheyenne land. As a result, many Southern Cheyenne sold their small farms in Oklahoma.

▲ *Members of a Southern Cheyenne family outside their home in the 1890s*

The Northern Cheyenne did not have this problem. Their reservation land was not open to outsiders. The tribe owned the land as a whole. It grazed cattle on the land, which brought money to the tribe.

▲ *Chief Two Moons speaks to a tribal meeting in 1913.*

After the 1930s, the U.S. government let Indian tribes become independent nations. As nations, they could ask the government for money and other aid. Reservation life began to slowly improve.

Modern Cheyenne

▲ *A tepee on the grounds of the Washita Battlefield National Historic Site near Cheyenne, Oklahoma*

Today's Cheyenne still have two reservations. They still call themselves Northern Cheyenne and Southern Cheyenne. Each group has its own tribal government.

The Cheyenne and the Arapaho of Oklahoma have eight members on their tribal **council**. They handle the tribe's business.

▲ *The Northern Cheyenne named a college after their famous chief, Dull Knife.*

They are in charge of the farms and ranches in the towns of Concho, Canton, and Colony. The tribe plants wheat and alfalfa. They raise cattle, buffalo, and hogs. The tribe also owns the Lucky Star Indian Casino in Concho.

The Northern Cheyenne have fourteen members on their tribal council. They oversee education, health, and law and order on their reservation. A college named after Chief Dull Knife is on the reservation.

▲ Senator and Northern Cheyenne Ben Nighthorse Campbell of Colorado and Senator Daniel Inouye of Hawaii at the groundbreaking ceremonies of the National Museum of the American Indian in Washington, D.C.

▲ *Dean Spotted Eagle, a Northern Cheyenne leader*

Today Cheyenne people live a modern life. They are improving their education and health care.

The Cheyenne share many of the same hopes and dreams as other Americans. They want good jobs and homes. They want their children to have better lives than they have.

The Cheyenne people also want to keep their language, history, and beliefs alive. Only then will their nation survive.

Glossary

ceremonies—formal actions to mark important times

council—a group of people chosen to make important decisions

fast—to go without food

Great Plains—the big prairies in the western United States and Canada

massacre—the killing of unarmed people

medicine bundle—a skin bag that holds sacred objects

raids—surprise attacks

reservation—large areas of land set aside for Native Americans; in Canada, reservations are called reserves

treaty—an agreement between two governments

warriors—people skilled in fighting battles

Did You Know?

- The Cheyenne used sign language to communicate with Native Americans who spoke another language.

- Cheyenne women made small cakes of dried buffalo meat, cornmeal, raisins, peanuts, and apples. They soaked the cakes in honey or maple syrup. The dish was called pemmican.

- The number of horses a Cheyenne family owned determined its wealth. Sometimes a herd included several hundred horses.

At a Glance

Tribal name: Tsistsistas

Divisions: Northern Cheyenne and Southern Cheyenne

Past locations: South Dakota, North Dakota, Colorado, Kansas, Minnesota, Montana, Nebraska, Oklahoma, Wyoming

Present locations: Montana, Oklahoma

Traditional houses: Earth lodge, tepee

Traditional clothing material: Skins

Traditional transportation: Horse

Traditional food: Corn, rice, beans, squash, fish, buffalo, foxes, squirrels

Important Dates

1680	The Cheyenne live along the Mississippi River in Minnesota.
1700s	The Cheyenne leave the Mississippi River valley in Minnesota and move west into the Dakotas.
1800s	The Cheyenne move west to Colorado, Wyoming, and Montana.
1832	The Cheyenne split into two groups—the Northern Cheyenne and the Southern Cheyenne.
1851	The Treaty of Fort Laramie is signed.
1864	The Sand Creek Massacre takes place.
1876	The Cheyenne and the Sioux beat General George Armstrong Custer in the Battle of the Little Bighorn.
1877	The Northern Cheyenne agree to go to the Cheyenne-Arapaho reservation in Oklahoma.
1881	The Northern Cheyenne get a reservation in Montana.
1934	Congress passes the Indian Reorganization Act, which gives Native Americans the right to govern themselves.
1992	Northern Cheyenne Ben Nighthorse Campbell is elected to the U.S. Senate.

At the Library

Hoig, Stan. *People of the Sacred Arrows: The Southern Cheyenne Today.* New York: Cobblehill Books, 1992.

Remington, Gwen. *The Cheyenne.* San Diego, Calif.: Lucent Books, 2001.

Sneve, Virginia Driving Hawk. *Cheyenne.* New York: Holiday House, 1996.

On the Web

Black Kettle

http://www.pbs.org/weta/thewest/people/a_c/blackkettle.htm
For more information about Cheyenne chief Black Kettle

The North American Indian: The Cheyenne

http://www.curtis-collection.com/tribe%20data/cheyenne.html
For essays and photographs by historian Edward S. Curtis

Through the Mail

Northern Cheyenne Tribal Council
P.O. Box 128
Lame Deer, MT 59043
To find out more information on Cheyenne history and government

On the Road

Heard Museum
2301 North Central Avenue
Phoenix, AZ 85004
602/252-8840
To learn more about the heritage, culture, and arts of the Cheyenne and other Native Americans

Index

About the Author

Petra Press is a freelance writer of young adult non-fiction, specializing in the diverse culture of the Americas. Her more than twenty books include histories of U.S. immigration, education, and settlement of the West, as well as portraits of numerous original cultures. She lives with her husband, David, in Milwaukee, Wisconsin.